CHRISTIAN
BASICS
BIBLE
STUDIES

Hope

NEVER BEYOND HOPE

J.I. Packer and Carolyn Nystrom

6 STUDIES FOR INDIVIDUALS OR GROUPS
WITH LEADER'S NOTES

Inter-Varsity Press
Nottingham, England

An imprint of InterVarsity Press
Downers Grove, Illinois

InterVarsity Press, USA
P.O. Box 1400, Downers Grove, IL 60515-1426
World Wide Web: www.ivpress.com
E-mail: email@ivpress.com

Inter-Varsity Press, England
Norton Street, Nottingham NG7 3HR, England
World Wide Web: www.ivpbooks.com
E-mail: ivp@ivpbooks.com

InterVarsity Press®, U.S.A. is the book-publishing division of InterVarsity Christian Fellowship/USA®, a
student movement active on campus at hundreds of universities, colleges and schools of nursing in the United
States of America, and a member movement of the International Fellowship of Evangelical Students. For
information about local and regional activities, write Public Relations Dept., InterVarsity Christian Fellowship/
USA, 6400 Schroeder Rd., P.O. Box 7895, Madison, WI 53707-7895, or visit the IVCF website at
<www.intervarsity.org>.

This study guide is based on and adapts material from Never Beyond Hope by J. I. Packer and Carolyn Nystrom
©2000.

Inter-Varsity Press, England, is the book-publishing division of the Universities and Colleges Christian Fellowship
(formerly the Inter-Varsity Fellowship), a student movement linking Christian Unions in universities and colleges
throughout the United Kingdom and the Republic of Ireland, and a member movement of the International
Fellowship of Evangelical Students. For more information about local and national activities, write to UCCF, 38
De Montfort Street, Leicester LE1 7GP, or visit the UCCF website at www.uccf.org.uk.

Cover design: Cindy Kiple; cover image: Andrew Judd/Masterfile

USA ISBN 978-0-8308-2017-7
UK ISBN 978-0-85111-355-5

Printed in the United States of America ∞

P   20   19   18   17   16   15   14   13   12   11   10   9   8   7   6
Y   21   20   19   18   17   16   15   14   13   12   11

CONTENTS

CONTENTS

Christian Basics Bible Studies

Knowing Christ is where faith begins. From there we grow through the essentials of discipleship: Bible study, prayer, Christian community and much more. We learn to set godly priorities, grow in Christian character and witness to others. We persevere through doubts and grow in wisdom. These are the topics woven into each of the Christian Basics Bible Studies. Working through this series will help you become a more mature Christian.

WHAT KIND OF GUIDE IS THIS?

The studies are not designed to merely tell you what one person thinks. Instead, through inductive study, they will help you discover for yourself what Scripture is saying. Each study deals with a particular passage—rather than jumping around the Bible—so that you can really delve into the author's meaning in that context.

The studies ask three different kinds of questions. *Observation* questions help you to understand the content of the passage by asking about the basic facts: who, what, when, where and how. *Interpretation* questions delve into the meaning of the passage. *Application* questions help you discover its implications for growing in Christ.

These three keys unlock the treasures of the biblical writings and help you live them out.

This is a thought-provoking guide. Each question assumes a variety of answers. Many questions do not have "right" answers, particularly questions that aim at meaning or application. Instead, the questions should inspire users to explore the passage more thoroughly.

This study guide is flexible. You can use it for individual study, but it is also great for a variety of groups—student, professional, neighborhood or church groups. Each study takes about forty-five minutes in a group setting or thirty minutes in personal study.

HOW THEY'RE PUT TOGETHER

Each study is composed of four sections: opening paragraphs and questions to help you get into the topic, the NIV text and questions that invite study of the passage, questions to help you apply what you have learned, and a suggestion for prayer.

The workbook format provides space for writing a response to each question. This format is ideal for personal study and allows group members to prepare in advance for the discussion and/or write down notes during the study. This space can form a permanent record of your thoughts and spiritual progress.

At the back of the guide are study notes that may be useful for leaders or for individuals. These notes do not give "the answers," but they do provide additional background information on certain questions to help you through the difficult spots. The "Guidelines for Leaders" section describes how to lead a group discussion, gives helpful tips on group dynamics and suggests ways to deal with problems that may arise during the discussion. With such helps, someone with little or no experience can lead an effective group study.

SUGGESTIONS FOR INDIVIDUAL STUDY

1. This guide is based on a classic book or booklet that will enrich your spiritual life. If you have not read the book or booklet suggested in the "Further Reading" section, you may want to read the portion suggested before you begin your study. The ideas in the book will enhance your study, but the Bible text will be the focus of each session.

2. Read the introduction. Consider the opening questions and note your responses.

3. Pray, asking God to speak to you from his Word about this particular topic.

4. Read the passage reproduced for you from the New International Version. You may wish to mark phrases that seem important. Note in the margin any questions that come to your mind as you read.

5. Use the questions from the study guide to more thoroughly examine the passage. Note your findings in the space provided. After you have made your own notes, read the corresponding study notes in the back of the book for further insights.

6. Reread the entire passage, making further notes about its general principles and about the way you intend to use them.

7. Move to the "Commit" section. Spend time prayerfully considering what the passage has to say specifically to your life.

8. Read the suggestion for prayer. Speak to God about insights you have gained. Tell him of any desires you have for specific growth. Ask him to help you as you attempt to live out the principles described in that passage.

SUGGESTIONS FOR MEMBERS OF A GROUP STUDY

Joining a Bible study group can be a great avenue to spiritual growth. Here are a few guidelines that will help you as you participate in the studies in this guide.

1. Reading the book suggested as further reading, before or after each session, will enhance your study and understanding of the themes in this guide.

2. These studies focus on a particular passage of Scripture—in depth. Only rarely should you refer to other portions of the Bible, and then only at the request of the leader. Of course, the Bible is internally consistent. Other good forms of study draw on that consistency, but inductive Bible study sticks with a single passage and works on it in depth.

3. These are discussion studies. Questions in this guide aim at helping a group discuss together a passage of Scripture in order to understand its content, meaning and implications. Most people are either natural talkers or natural listeners, yet this type of study works best if people participate more or less evenly. Try to curb any natural tendency to either excessive talking or excessive quiet. You and the rest of the group will benefit.

4. Most questions in this guide allow for a variety of answers. If you disagree with someone else's comment, gently say so. Then explain your own point of view from the passage before you.

5. Be willing to lead a discussion, if asked. Much of the preparation for leading has already been accomplished in the writing of this guide.

6. Respect the privacy of people in your group. Many people speak

of things within the context of a Bible study/prayer group that they do not want to be public knowledge. Assume that personal information spoken within the group setting is private, unless you are specifically told otherwise. And don't talk about it elsewhere.

7. We recommend that all groups follow a few basic guidelines and that these guidelines be read at the first session. The guidelines, which you may wish to adapt to your situation, are the following:

a. Anything said in this group is considered confidential and will not be discussed outside the group unless specific permission is given to do so.

b. We will provide time for each person present to talk if he or she feels comfortable doing so.

c. We will talk about ourselves and our own situations, avoiding conversation about other people.

d. We will listen attentively to each other.

e. We will pray for each other.

8. Enjoy your study. Prepare to grow.

SUGGESTIONS FOR GROUP LEADERS

There are specific suggestions to help you in leading in the "Guidelines for Leaders" and in the "Study Notes" at the back of this guide. Read the "Guidelines for Leaders" carefully, even if you are only leading one group meeting. Then you can go to the section on the particular session you will lead.

INTRODUCTION
Never Beyond Hope

M ay the God of hope fill you with all joy and peace as you trust in him, so that you may overflow with hope by the power of the Holy Spirit" (Romans 15:13). This prayer of blessing comes near the end of the Apostle Paul's great letter to Christians in Rome. Can we, his present-day readers, receive that blessing of hope?

We can indeed. But many of us live under the weight of our own failures. We know, all too well, our flaws and they rob us of hope. Some of us are burdened with a crushing sense of inferiority. We run scared, afraid of being caught in some folly that we failed to notice. Some of us bear the scars of pain we cannot forget and damage we cannot repair. For some, guilty memories keep shame and self-contempt alive in our hearts. Some feel imprisoned in a loveless home or a soul-destroying routine that encourages us to resent our very existence. In these troubling settings, emotional exhaustion leaves our faith as fragile as tissue paper. Hoping for anything is simply beyond us.

The final answer to this flawed condition of hopelessness is that God loves, redeems, pardons, restores, protects, keeps and uses misfits, outsiders and failures. Scripture shows God using the oddest, rawest, most lopsided and flawed of his children to further his work, while at the same time he carries on his sanctifying strategy for getting them into better moral and spiritual shape. For sensitive souls who feel they are not fit to serve God, this is a fact of enormous encouragement.

We see God deal with Jacob the cheat; diffident Mrs. Manoah; Jonah the pig-headed patriot; bossy, noisy Martha and quiet, passive Mary; Thomas the stupid-smart professional pessimist; and impulsive, warm-hearted, unstable Simon Peter. God blessed and used these people—even as he led them forward out of the bondage of their own defects into truer godliness than they had previously thought possible. And God wants to do the same with each of us.

Do we need hope? Yes. Can Christians hope? Yes. Are we ever beyond hope? No! Does our hope of salvation bring joy, energy, faithfulness and a desire to be of use to God? Yes, yes, yes, yes. May we hope that God will use us each day to his glory, even though we are not as yet perfectly sanctified? Yes. Is this glorious good news? Yes.

Good hoping to you—or as some say, here's hoping!—hoping as a way of life, hoping as a source of strength and hoping as a fountain of joy in the heart from which praise and prayer will flow out continually.

S T U D Y   O N E

Jacob:
Hope for the Unhappy
Genesis 32:1-32

When Jacob was born, he came out of his mother's womb with his hand holding on to his twin brother's heel. Getting ahead was Jacob's consistent goal. When the twins neared adulthood, Jacob first persuaded Esau, his elder brother (elder by minutes), to sell him his birthright. Then he also stole Esau's blessing. To which Esau said, "This is too much! I'd like to kill that brother of mine. In due course, I will." And Rebekah, their mother, said to Jacob, "You'd better leave, or else." So off went Jacob, who spent twenty years with Uncle Laban.

As we go through the story of Jacob the adult, we find that in many ways he lived up to his name. He was something of a grabber, an exploiter, a manipulator and a cheat. None of this brought Jacob happiness; instead, it brought tension, strain and ill will. Only when his passion for gain was finally put second to his passion for God did his life settle down. That was after Jacob tried for many years to be both worldly and godly, on the make and under the mercy, a course of action that led to the crisis at Jabbok—the turning point of his whole existence.

But there's more to the story than this. The other side of Jacob's character, from the time we meet him, is that with his heart for gain, he also had a heart for God, given him by God himself—God who always takes the initiative in grace. God wanted Jacob as his man, and Jacob wanted God as his God.

OPEN

- What do you see of yourself in Jacob?

- What are some ways that you have looked for happiness—and failed to find it?

STUDY

Read Genesis 32.

¹Jacob also went on his way, and the angels of God met him. ²When Jacob saw them, he said, "This is the camp of God!" So he named that place Mahanaim.

³Jacob sent messengers ahead of him to his brother Esau in the land of Seir, the country of Edom. ⁴He instructed them: "This is what you are to say to my master Esau: 'Your servant Jacob says, I have been staying with Laban and have remained there till now. ⁵I have cattle and donkeys, sheep and goats, menservants and maid-

servants. Now I am sending this message to my lord, that I may find favor in your eyes.'"

⁶When the messengers returned to Jacob, they said, "We went to your brother Esau, and now he is coming to meet you, and four hundred men are with him."

⁷In great fear and distress Jacob divided the people who were with him into two groups, and the flocks and herds and camels as well. ⁸He thought, "If Esau comes and attacks one group, the group that is left may escape."

⁹Then Jacob prayed, "O God of my father Abraham, God of my father Isaac, O LORD, who said to me, 'Go back to your country and your relatives, and I will make you prosper,' ¹⁰I am unworthy of all the kindness and faithfulness you have shown your servant. I had only my staff when I crossed this Jordan, but now I have become two groups. ¹¹Save me, I pray, from the hand of my brother Esau, for I am afraid he will come and attack me, and also the mothers with their children. ¹²But you have said, 'I will surely make you prosper and will make your descendants like the sand of the sea, which cannot be counted.'"

¹³He spent the night there, and from what he had with him he selected a gift for his brother Esau: ¹⁴two hundred female goats and twenty male goats, two hundred ewes and twenty rams, ¹⁵thirty female camels with their young, forty cows and ten bulls, and twenty female donkeys and ten male donkeys. ¹⁶He put them in the care of his servants, each herd by itself, and said to his servants, "Go ahead of me, and keep some space between the herds."

¹⁷He instructed the one in the lead: "When my brother Esau meets you and asks, 'To whom do you belong, and where are you going, and who owns all these animals in front of you?' ¹⁸then you are to say, 'They belong to your servant Jacob. They are a gift sent to my lord Esau, and he is coming behind us.'"

[19]He also instructed the second, the third and all the others who followed the herds: "You are to say the same thing to Esau when you meet him. [20]And be sure to say, 'Your servant Jacob is coming behind us.' " For he thought, "I will pacify him with these gifts I am sending on ahead; later, when I see him, perhaps he will receive me." [21]So Jacob's gifts went on ahead of him, but he himself spent the night in the camp.

[22]That night Jacob got up and took his two wives, his two maidservants and his eleven sons and crossed the ford of the Jabbok. [23]After he had sent them across the stream, he sent over all his possessions. [24]So Jacob was left alone, and a man wrestled with him till daybreak. [25]When the man saw that he could not overpower him, he touched the socket of Jacob's hip so that his hip was wrenched as he wrestled with the man. [26]Then the man said, "Let me go, for it is daybreak."

But Jacob replied, "I will not let you go unless you bless me."

[27]The man asked him, "What is your name?"

"Jacob," he answered.

[28]Then the man said, "Your name will no longer be Jacob, but Israel, because you have struggled with God and with men and have overcome."

[29]Jacob said, "Please tell me your name."

But he replied, "Why do you ask my name?" Then he blessed him there.

[30]So Jacob called the place Peniel, saying, "It is because I saw God face to face, and yet my life was spared."

[31]The sun rose above him as he passed Peniel, and he was limping because of his hip. [32]Therefore to this day the Israelites do not eat the tendon attached to the socket of the hip, because the socket of Jacob's hip was touched near the tendon.

1. What precautions did Jacob take that might lead to a peaceful meeting with his brother (vv. 1-21)?

2. Study Jacob's prayer in verses 9-12. What do the various phrases of his prayer suggest about his relationship with God?

3. Focus on verses 22-32. In what way was this encounter with God different from the relationship suggested by his prayer?

4. In what ways do you think Jacob would have been different after his encounter with God?

5. If you were to have a wrestling match with God, what would it likely be about?

6. God reveals himself in ways most important to the person he meets—as he did to Jacob. How has God revealed himself in a way that was particularly appropriate for you?

7. Jacob limped, probably all of his life, after his encounter with God. In view of what you know of Jacob's life thus far, how was this limp likely to influence the person he was becoming?

8. What could Jacob have learned about God as a result of this trip?

9. How might Jacob's encounter with God encourage you in your own periods of unhappiness?

 COMMIT

Divide Jacob's prayer of Genesis 32:9-12 into four parts, and use it as an outline for your own praying.

Verse 9: Talk to God about your own past experiences with him, particularly as it relates to your family. Bring to him the current work that he has placed in your hand.

Verse 10. Give thanks to God for all that he has given you, acknowledging that these gifts and skills did not come by your own efforts alone. Express praise for God's character and your own need and dependence on him.

Verse 11. Bring to God your most serious current problem. Be honest about your fears and any sense of inadequacy. Ask for his intervention to bring about what is right and good.

Verse 12. Remind God (and yourself) of his promises to you. See, for example, Isaiah 41:9-10.

We serve a God who loves us, and we're to interpret everything that happens to us in terms of the love of God. Jacob was in the process of learning this life concept. Meditate on that sentence as it relates to the events in your own life. As you recall events of joy, satisfaction and pain, write an honest response of prayer to God.

For further reading: *Chapter two of* Never Beyond Hope.

S T U D Y   T W O

Manoah's Wife: Hope for the Ignored
Judges 13:1-25

Mrs. Manoah, as we have to call her because we are told only the name of her husband, is quiet and ordinarily stays in the background. She lives with constant putdowns that flow from Manoah's unwillingness to trust other people. When an angelic visitor appears to her (not her husband), she is scared, but she listens carefully. Next she goes straight to her husband to whom she reports the visitor's message with perfect accuracy. Manoah's assumption is that he cannot rely on her account. But God has a surprise for both of them.

It is God's way to spring surprises in the lives of his people. Now imagine yourself standing alongside Manoah and his wife and watching that happen. The visitor who first spoke to Mrs. Manoah has returned. This time she is able to call her husband so that Manoah can hear the message himself. Suddenly the visitor who a moment ago was beside them has somehow moved into the flame of a burned offering. He's literally going up in it. And now he's vanished, which they found traumatic—especially Manoah.

This was God in action. From that event we immediately learn that knowing God is not just a matter of doctrinal understanding, of thoroughgoing commitment, of personal, disciplined communion with God or of peaceful contentment in God (although it includes all those things). It isn't just a matter of focusing on Christ as the way to God as your Savior—though it includes that too. With and beyond all that has been mentioned, knowing God is a matter of being ready for surprises. And quiet, shy, ignored Mrs. Manoah was ready for the unpredictability of God. She was a great woman! A woman honored, sustained and used by God.

 OPEN

■ What are some ways that you respond to unexpected events?

■ When I am ignored

___ I shrink further back into the corners

___ I make myself impossible to ignore

___ I watch, listen and see what I can learn

___ I feel hurt, angry and worthless

_X_ My response depends on the situation (Explain)
IS IT ABOUT ME OR SOMEONE ELSE

 STUDY

Read Judges 13:1-25.

[1]Again the Israelites did evil in the eyes of the LORD, so the LORD delivered them into the hands of the Philistines for forty years.

[2]A certain man of Zorah, named Manoah, from the clan of the Danites, had a wife who was sterile and remained childless. [3]The angel of the LORD appeared to her and said, "You are sterile and child-

less, but you are going to conceive and have a son. ⁴Now see to it that you drink no wine or other fermented drink and that you do not eat anything unclean, ⁵because you will conceive and give birth to a son. No razor may be used on his head, because the boy is to be a Nazirite, set apart to God from birth, and he will begin the deliverance of Israel from the hands of the Philistines."

⁶Then the woman went to her husband and told him, "A man of God came to me. He looked like an angel of God, very awesome. I didn't ask him where he came from, and he didn't tell me his name. ⁷But he said to me, 'You will conceive and give birth to a son. Now then, drink no wine or other fermented drink and do not eat anything unclean, because the boy will be a Nazirite of God from birth until the day of his death.'"

⁸Then Manoah prayed to the LORD: "O Lord, I beg you, let the man of God you sent to us come again to teach us how to bring up the boy who is to be born."

⁹God heard Manoah, and the angel of God came again to the woman while she was out in the field; but her husband Manoah was not with her. ¹⁰The woman hurried to tell her husband, "He's here! The man who appeared to me the other day!"

¹¹Manoah got up and followed his wife. When he came to the man, he said, "Are you the one who talked to my wife?"

"I am," he said.

¹²So Manoah asked him, "When your words are fulfilled, what is to be the rule for the boy's life and work?"

¹³The angel of the LORD answered, "Your wife must do all that I have told her. ¹⁴She must not eat anything that comes from the grapevine, nor drink any wine or other fermented drink nor eat anything unclean. She must do everything I have commanded her."

¹⁵Manoah said to the angel of the LORD, "We would like you to

stay until we prepare a young goat for you."

¹⁶The angel of the LORD replied, "Even though you detain me, I will not eat any of your food. But if you prepare a burnt offering, offer it to the LORD." (Manoah did not realize that it was the angel of the LORD.)

¹⁷Then Manoah inquired of the angel of the LORD, "What is your name, so that we may honor you when your word comes true?"

¹⁸He replied, "Why do you ask my name? It is beyond understanding." ¹⁹Then Manoah took a young goat, together with the grain offering, and sacrificed it on a rock to the LORD. And the LORD did an amazing thing while Manoah and his wife watched: ²⁰As the flame blazed up from the altar toward heaven, the angel of the LORD ascended in the flame. Seeing this, Manoah and his wife fell with their faces to the ground. ²¹When the angel of the LORD did not show himself again to Manoah and his wife, Manoah realized that it was the angel of the LORD.

²²"We are doomed to die!" he said to his wife. "We have seen God!"

²³But his wife answered, "If the LORD had meant to kill us, he would not have accepted a burnt offering and grain offering from our hands, nor shown us all these things or now told us this."

²⁴The woman gave birth to a boy and named him Samson. He grew and the LORD blessed him, ²⁵and the Spirit of the LORD began to stir him while he was in Mahaneh Dan, between Zorah and Eshtaol.

---

1. In what ways would this visit from "the angel of God" change the lives of Manoah and his wife?

They saw God
DAILY eating habits changed
Became Kosher for sure
Became parents

2. What reasons did they have to be frightened about this visit?

They saw God!

to be joyful? *Son to come*

---

3. Why do you think the angel of God came to the woman both times?

She believed and was faithful

---

4. What does the conversation between the woman, the man and the angel reveal about the relationship between Manoah and his wife?

He believed her as far as it was rational

---

5. What hints of yourself do you see in Manoah?

Discounting God's voice in my life

in Mrs. Manoah?

Steadfast, persistent

---

6. Study verses 16-20. What can Manoah and his wife know about

God from this experience?

He relates to us patiently
His powers are beyond our understanding

---

7. God is a surprising God. What are some ways of God that you find mysterious?

Unfolding of his plans through worldly chaos

---

8. How might the story of Manoah and his wife help you cope with life's surprises?

Don't ignore miracles
Gifts come with work attached

 COMMIT

■ God blessed Manoah with a sensible and spiritually discerning wife. Who within your own circle of acquaintances possesses similar characteristics? How can you respectfully draw on those strengths?

Spiritually discerning wife
Jill, Nancy, Pat

"Why do you ask my name?" said the angel of the Lord, "It is beyond understanding." Pray, praising God for who he is—even for those aspects that you cannot fully understand.

For further reading: Chapter three of Never Beyond Hope.

obedience
compassion

Jonah:
Hope for the Angry
Jonah 1—4

The book of Jonah is about an angry man and his God, a merciless man and his merciful God. But even to say it that way is backward. The correct arrangement of Jonah's theme is that it's a story of our merciful God and his merciless man.

God teaches Jonah, the merciless man, two lessons that he badly needed to learn. The first lesson is one of obedience. God had called Jonah to be a prophet: a man charged to run God's errands and deliver God's messages. The story begins with Jonah refusing to obey. In the first two chapters God uses a great fish to teach him the lesson of obedience. But then there's a second lesson. Jonah is a hard man, stonehearted and merciless—and he has to learn the lesson of exchanging his anger for compassion. In the last two chapters we watch God teach him that using, this time, not a great fish but a little worm.

This is a story for all of us. God doesn't always pick the nice men and the nice women. In fact, it's just the opposite. It is God's way to choose and to use flawed human material. God picks sinners; God saves sinners; God calls, equips and uses sinners—and Jonah was one such sinner.

OPEN

■ When and how has your own anger gotten you in trouble?

■ What evidences have you seen of God's mercy? Bring to mind a situation where God granted you far more than you expected or deserved. Describe the situation and your feelings about it as much as possible.

STUDY

Read Jonah 1.

¹The word of the LORD came to Jonah son of Amittai: ²"Go to the great city of Nineveh and preach against it, because its wickedness has come up before me."

³But Jonah ran away from the LORD and headed for Tarshish. He went down to Joppa, where he found a ship bound for that port. After paying the fare, he went aboard and sailed for Tarshish to flee from the LORD.

⁴Then the LORD sent a great wind on the sea, and such a violent storm arose that the ship threatened to break up. ⁵All the sailors were afraid and each cried out to his own god. And they threw the cargo into the sea to lighten the ship.

But Jonah had gone below deck, where he lay down and fell into a deep sleep. ⁶The captain went to him and said, "How can you sleep?

Get up and call on your god! Maybe he will take notice of us, and we will not perish."

[7]Then the sailors said to each other, "Come, let us cast lots to find out who is responsible for this calamity." They cast lots and the lot fell on Jonah.

[8]So they asked him, "Tell us, who is responsible for making all this trouble for us? What do you do? Where do you come from? What is your country? From what people are you?"

[9]He answered, "I am a Hebrew and I worship the LORD, the God of heaven, who made the sea and the land."

[10]This terrified them and they asked, "What have you done?" (They knew he was running away from the LORD, because he had already told them so.)

[11]The sea was getting rougher and rougher. So they asked him, "What should we do to you to make the sea calm down for us?"

[12]"Pick me up and throw me into the sea," he replied, "and it will become calm. I know that it is my fault that this great storm has come upon you."

[13]Instead, the men did their best to row back to land. But they could not, for the sea grew even wilder than before. [14]Then they cried to the LORD, "O LORD, please do not let us die for taking this man's life. Do not hold us accountable for killing an innocent man, for you, O LORD, have done as you pleased." [15]Then they took Jonah and threw him overboard, and the raging sea grew calm. [16]At this the men greatly feared the LORD, and they offered a sacrifice to the LORD and made vows to him.

[17]But the LORD provided a great fish to swallow Jonah, and Jonah was inside the fish three days and three nights.

Read Jonah 2:1, 10.

[1]From inside the fish Jonah prayed to the LORD his God. . . .

¹⁰And the L**ORD** commanded the fish, and it vomited Jonah onto dry land.

Read Jonah 3.

¹Then the word of the L**ORD** came to Jonah a second time: ²"Go to the great city of Nineveh and proclaim to it the message I give you."

³Jonah obeyed the word of the L**ORD** and went to Nineveh. Now Nineveh was a very important city—a visit required three days. ⁴On the first day, Jonah started into the city. He proclaimed: "Forty more days and Nineveh will be overturned." ⁵The Ninevites believed God. They declared a fast, and all of them, from the greatest to the least, put on sackcloth. ⁶When the news reached the king of Nineveh, he rose from his throne, took off his royal robes, covered himself with sackcloth and sat down in the dust. ⁷Then he issued a proclamation in Nineveh:

"By the decree of the king and his nobles:

Do not let any man or beast, herd or flock, taste anything; do not let them eat or drink. ⁸But let man and beast be covered with sackcloth. Let everyone call urgently on God. Let them give up their evil ways and their violence. ⁹Who knows? God may yet relent and with compassion turn from his fierce anger so that we will not perish."

¹⁰When God saw what they did and how they turned from their evil ways, he had compassion and did not bring upon them the destruction he had threatened.

Read Jonah 4:1-2, 10-11.

¹But Jonah was greatly displeased and became angry. ²He prayed to the L**ORD**, "O L**ORD**, is this not what I said when I was still at home? That is why I was so quick to flee to Tarshish. I knew that you are a gracious and compassionate God, slow to anger and abounding

in love, a God who relents from sending calamity." . . . [10]But the
LORD said, "You have been concerned about this vine, though you
did not tend it or make it grow. It sprang up overnight and died overnight. [11]But Nineveh has more than a hundred and twenty thousand
people who cannot tell their right hand from their left, and many
cattle as well. Should I not be concerned about that great city?"

---

1. What actions reveal Jonah's character?

   What do you see of yourself in Jonah?

---

2. What examples do you see of the grace of God in Jonah's story?

---

3. Study Jonah's two descriptions of God in 1:9 and 4:2. In what
   ways did Jonah act on these stated beliefs?

   In what ways did his actions fail to live up to his beliefs?

4. Reread each of these descriptions of God with your own current circumstances in mind. What actions can you take that would live out this belief?

_____

5. How was the fish helpful to Jonah?

_____

6. When has a break in your routine given you valuable insights from God?

_____

7. In spite of Jonah's anger and other flaws, what good did God accomplish through him?

_____

8. Jonah needed to learn two lessons: the lesson of obedience and the lesson of compassion. What measures did God use to teach those lessons?

9. How might you put one of Jonah's lessons to work in your own setting?

 COMMIT

■ Spend a few moments in silence, reflecting on the life of Jonah. Ask God to reveal to you what he would like you to glean from Jonah's experience.

■ Jonah's time inside a fish gave him opportunity to block out all distractions and get honest with God. (Most of us don't need a near drowning to experience this.) Create your own "fish" by purposely finding a time and place to communicate privately with God. Ask him to search your heart about the current direction of your life. (Are you appropriately obedient to God? Compassionate to others—even those you don't like?) Write out your prayer and meditation.

Jonah complained in 4:2, "I knew that you are a gracious and compassionate God, slow to anger and abounding in love, a God who relents from sending calamity." Pray, talking to God about your own response to these aspects of his character.

For further reading: Chapter four of Never Beyond Hope.

Martha:
Hope for the Overworked

Luke 10:38-42; John 11:1-44; 12:1-3

Martha the sister of Mary is naturally a take-charge person, a manager by instinct. We meet Martha first as a hostess. Jesus, we are told, came to a village where a woman named Martha opened her home to him (Luke 10:38).

It's Martha's home. That probably means that Martha is a widow, because under ordinary circumstances in ancient Palestine a woman wouldn't own property—but the widow regularly did. Martha has a sister named Mary, who lives with her, and a brother named Lazarus, who also seems to live in the same home. On this day Martha heard a knock at the door, went to see who it was and found thirteen unexpected guests: Jesus and his twelve disciples. What does a good hostess do when she finds guests on the doorstep? Without making it obvious that this is a bit of a shock, she takes a deep breath and says, "Why, how nice to see you all. Come in."

Soon Jesus turns their rest hour into a teaching session. I suppose he sits rabbi-like, on a chair in the center of a semicircle of his disciples—or maybe they're all sitting on the floor. Mary tiptoes in and sits down at one end of the semicircle while Martha squares her shoulders and heads for the kitchen.

OPEN

- Who is one of the favorite Marthas in your life, and what do you appreciate about that person?

- When and how have you benefited by knowing (or being) a Mary?

STUDY

Read Luke 10:38-42.

[38]As Jesus and his disciples were on their way, he came to a village where a woman named Martha opened her home to him. [39]She had a sister called Mary, who sat at the Lord's feet listening to what he said. [40]But Martha was distracted by all the preparations that had to be made. She came to him and asked, "Lord, don't you care that my sister has left me to do the work by myself? Tell her to help me!"

[41]"Martha, Martha," the Lord answered, "you are worried and upset about many things, [42]but only one thing is needed. Mary has chosen what is better, and it will not be taken away from her."

Read John 11:1-44.

[1]Now a man named Lazarus was sick. He was from Bethany, the village of Mary and her sister Martha. . . . [5]Jesus loved Martha and her sister and Lazarus. [6]Yet when he heard that Lazarus was sick, he stayed where he was two more days.

[7]Then he said to his disciples, "Let us go back to Judea." . . .

[17]On his arrival, Jesus found that Lazarus had already been in the tomb for four days. [18]Bethany was less than two miles from Jerusalem, [19]and many Jews had come to Martha and Mary to comfort them in the loss of their brother. [20]When Martha heard that Jesus was coming, she went out to meet him, but Mary stayed at home.

[21]"Lord," Martha said to Jesus, "if you had been here, my brother would not have died. [22]But I know that even now God will give you whatever you ask."

[23]Jesus said to her, "Your brother will rise again."

[24]Martha answered, "I know he will rise again in the resurrection at the last day."

[25]Jesus said to her, "I am the resurrection and the life. He who believes in me will live, even though he dies; [26]and whoever lives and believes in me will never die. Do you believe this?"

[27]"Yes, Lord," she told him, "I believe that you are the Christ, the Son of God, who was to come into the world."

[28]And after she had said this, she went back and called her sister Mary aside. "The Teacher is here," she said, "and is asking for you." . . . [38]Jesus, once more deeply moved, came to the tomb. It was a cave with a stone laid across the entrance. [39]"Take away the stone," he said.

"But, Lord," said Martha, the sister of the dead man, "by this time there is a bad odor, for he has been there four days."

[40]Then Jesus said, "Did I not tell you that if you believed, you would see the glory of God?"

[41]So they took away the stone. Then Jesus looked up and said, "Father, I thank you that you have heard me. [42]I knew that you always hear me, but I said this for the benefit of the people standing here, that they may believe that you sent me."

[43]When he had said this, Jesus called in a loud voice, "Lazarus, come out!" [44]The dead man came out, his hands and feet wrapped

with strips of linen, and a cloth around his face.

Jesus said to them, "Take off the grave clothes and let him go."

Read John 12:1-3.

[1]Six days before the Passover, Jesus arrived at Bethany, where Lazarus lived, whom Jesus had raised from the dead. [2]Here a dinner was given in Jesus' honor. Martha served, while Lazarus was among those reclining at the table with him. [3]Then Mary took about a pint of pure nard, an expensive perfume; she poured it on Jesus' feet and wiped his feet with her hair. And the house was filled with the fragrance of the perfume.

---

1. In Luke 10:38-42 Martha's complaint about her sister took three forms: "Lord, don't you care?" "My sister has left me to do the work." "Tell her to help me." What do each of Martha's complaints suggest about her need to grow as a disciple of Jesus?

---

2. How does Jesus, in his response, use each complaint to guide Martha toward being a better disciple?

---

3. What scenes from the story in John 11 stand out in your mind?

4. Look at John 11:5-6. Why do you think Jesus stayed where he was after hearing Lazarus was sick?

5. Focus on John 11:17-26. What steps led Martha to her statement of faith in verse 27?

6. Slowly and thoughtfully read Jesus' words about himself in John 11:25-26. In what particular situations do these words bring you hope?

7. Read John 12:1-3. What expressions of discipleship to Jesus do you see here?

8. As you observe the way each of the three siblings expressed their

devotion to Jesus in these verses, which is closest to your own natural expression? How?

---

9. Most people are naturally inclined to express their commitment to Jesus in the practical work of Martha or the passionate devotion of Mary. We all need to learn to be both Mary and Martha—at different times. What steps could you take to develop better discipleship in your weaker area?

 COMMIT

■ In God's presence examine your motives for specific acts of service. Are you really looking for recognition and reward? Are you, like Martha, frustrated when people do not take note of your hard work? (Or have you failed to express appreciation for the work of others?) Ask God to purify your motives. Acknowledge that your Lord sees and your Lord cares—regardless of the response of others.

Pray, meditating on each phrase of Christ's declaration and Martha's confession in John 11:25-27. Use each phrase as a launch for your own prayer on that subject.

For further reading: *Chapter five of* Never Beyond Hope.

Thomas:
Hope for the
Hard to Convince
John 20:19-31

Thomas said, "Unless I see the nail marks in his hands and put my finger where the nails were, and put my hand into his side, I will not believe it" (John 20:25). Thomas just couldn't believe that the other ten disciples had seen the Lord the way they had told him they had. What an extraordinary way for Thomas to behave!

This was the evening of the day that changed the world. Jesus, who had died as a sacrifice for our sins, rose from the dead, and showed himself alive and well on planet Earth.

The disciples had been huddled behind locked doors. The Jewish leaders had recently disposed of their Master, and now the disciples were afraid that the same people would be after them. Yes, the tomb had been found empty earlier that morning, but it was women who found it—and it wasn't the way of first-century Jewish men to take too seriously things that women told them.

Suddenly through the locked door, somehow (they never knew how), came the risen Jesus in his resurrected body. He spoke, and his first words were "Peace be with you." I think he spoke the words slowly so that the disciples would think about their meaning. And when he said this, we're told he showed them his hands and his side. He did it so they would see the wounds and be reminded of how he'd suffered to bring peace to them. He then commissioned them. They were to be his messengers in the world from that point on. "As the Father has sent me, I am sending you." Next came an odd gesture. He breathed on them. It was an act of prophecy of what was to happen at Pentecost. "Receive the Holy Spirit," he said.

All of this happened when Thomas wasn't there.

OPEN

- Would you say that Thomas's skepticism in this situation was bad or good? Why?

STUDY

Read John 20:19-31.

[19]On the evening of that first day of the week, when the disciples were together, with the doors locked for fear of the Jews, Jesus came and stood among them and said, "Peace be with you!" [20]After he said this, he showed them his hands and side. The disciples were overjoyed when they saw the Lord.

[21]Again Jesus said, "Peace be with you! As the Father has sent me, I am sending you." [22]And with that he breathed on them and said, "Receive the Holy Spirit. [23]If you forgive anyone his sins, they are forgiven; if you do not forgive them, they are not forgiven."

[24]Now Thomas (called Didymus), one of the Twelve, was not with

the disciples when Jesus came. [25]So the other disciples told him, "We have seen the Lord!"

But he said to them, "Unless I see the nail marks in his hands and put my finger where the nails were, and put my hand into his side, I will not believe it."

[26]A week later his disciples were in the house again, and Thomas was with them. Though the doors were locked, Jesus came and stood among them and said, "Peace be with you!" [27]Then he said to Thomas, "Put your finger here; see my hands. Reach out your hand and put it into my side. Stop doubting and believe."

[28]Thomas said to him, "My Lord and my God!"

[29]Then Jesus told him, "Because you have seen me, you have believed; blessed are those who have not seen and yet have believed."

[30]Jesus did many other miraculous signs in the presence of his disciples, which are not recorded in this book. [31]But these are written that you may believe that Jesus is the Christ, the Son of God, and that by believing you may have life in his name.

---

1. Why were the various events recorded in verses 19-23 important to Thomas and the other disciples?

---

2. Imagine yourself in Thomas's sandals at the second meeting, and trace the words and events as he sees them. What changes take place in his thoughts and emotions?

3. What all is included in Thomas's statement, "My Lord and my God!" (v. 28)?

4. Thomas was dealing with several possible obstacles to faith, among them temperament, stress, pride and resentment. When and how has one of these forces made it hard for you to believe in Jesus?

5. When you have had moments of doubt or skepticism about Christianity, what questions came to your mind?

6. In verses 30-31, John shares with his readers his reason for writing the book of John, his eyewitness account of the life, death and resurrection of Jesus. He says, "These are written that you may believe."

Our belief bridges the centuries and joins Thomas in his faith. What specific form should our faith take—according to these verses?

7. What evidences of Christ's resurrection do you find most convincing?

8. Jesus blessed Thomas but he also blesses our long-distance faith. "Because you have seen me, you have believed; blessed are those who have not seen and yet have believed" (verse 29). When and how have you responded to this invitation? If this has not yet occurred in your life, what steps toward faith are you willing to take now?

9. Convinced, Thomas said to Jesus, "My Lord and my God." Are you able to make that same statement? If so, what does that mean in what you believe about Jesus? In how you pray? In how you live? (Be as specific as possible.)

COMMIT

- Think through your own doubts about the Christian faith. In the presence of God confront these. Ask him to enlarge your understanding, to give you faith to believe even what you cannot see or touch. Place yourself under Christ's blessing: "Blessed are those who have not seen and yet have believed."

- Jesus said in John 14:6, "I am the way and the truth and the life. No one comes to the Father except through me." Write of some attempts you have made to find a way, truth or life by some other route. Then write of how Jesus has become the way, truth and life to you.

Thomas prayed a prayer of commitment to Jesus: "My Lord and my God." Pray your own prayer expressing to God your own level of faith and commitment.

For further reading: *Chapter six of* Never Beyond Hope.

Simon Peter: Hope When I Have Done Something Terrible
John 21:1-25; 1 Peter 5:8-11

Simon son of John, do you truly love me?" That was Jesus' searching question for Simon Peter, and it's an equally searching question for you and me. Jesus put it to Peter three times in as many minutes. We who claim to be his disciples today should think of him as putting it to us at every turn of the road in our life journey.

Peter was a natural leader. He ran his own fishing business, and he was the kind of confident, warm-hearted, outgoing person who assumes command in every situation. For instance, look at the occasion at Caesarea Philippi recorded in Matthew 16:13-19. Jesus said, "Who do people say the Son of Man is?" After the disciples had replied that different people were saying different things, Jesus came back at them and said, "But . . . who do you say that I am?" He was asking all of them, but it was Peter who spoke up and gave an answer for them: "You are the Christ, the Son of the living God."

From these and other events recorded throughout the four Gospels we can see that Jesus, right from the start, saw Peter as spiritual leader and prepared him for that role. But the story of Peter's discipleship before the cross ends with real spiritual disaster. Three times Peter denies that he knows Jesus, that he's ever had anything to do with Jesus, that there's any substance to the idea that he might be a disciple of Jesus. Near dawn Peter hears the voice of a rooster opening the day, realizes what he's done and is devastated. He went out and wept bitterly. And who can wonder? He had said, "Though all the rest of them should disown you, I won't!" But now he hears the cock crow. He realizes that disowning Jesus is precisely what he's done.

OPEN

■ Summarize Peter's positive and negative qualities as a disciple.

■ What do you see of yourself in Peter?

STUDY
Read John 21.

[1]Jesus appeared again to his disciples, by the Sea of Tiberias. It happened this way: [2]Simon Peter, Thomas (called Didymus), Nathanael from Cana in Galilee, the sons of Zebedee, and two other disciples were together. [3]"I'm going out to fish," Simon Peter told them, and they said, "We'll go with you." So they went out and got into the boat, but that night they caught nothing.

[4]Early in the morning, Jesus stood on the shore, but the disciples did not realize that it was Jesus.

[5]He called out to them, "Friends, haven't you any fish?"

"No," they answered.

⁶He said, "Throw your net on the right side of the boat and you will find some." When they did, they were unable to haul the net in because of the large number of fish.

⁷Then the disciple whom Jesus loved said to Peter, "It is the Lord!" As soon as Simon Peter heard him say, "It is the Lord," he wrapped his outer garment around him (for he had taken it off) and jumped into the water. ⁸The other disciples followed in the boat, towing the net full of fish, for they were not far from shore, about a hundred yards. ⁹When they landed, they saw a fire of burning coals there with fish on it, and some bread.

¹⁰Jesus said to them, "Bring some of the fish you have just caught."

¹¹Simon Peter climbed aboard and dragged the net ashore. It was full of large fish, 153, but even with so many the net was not torn. ¹²Jesus said to them, "Come and have breakfast." None of the disciples dared ask him, "Who are you?" They knew it was the Lord. ¹³Jesus came, took the bread and gave it to them, and did the same with the fish. ¹⁴This was now the third time Jesus appeared to his disciples after he was raised from the dead.

¹⁵When they had finished eating, Jesus said to Simon Peter, "Simon son of John, do you truly love me more than these?"

"Yes, Lord," he said, "you know that I love you."

Jesus said, "Feed my lambs."

¹⁶Again Jesus said, "Simon son of John, do you truly love me?"

He answered, "Yes, Lord, you know that I love you."

Jesus said, "Take care of my sheep."

¹⁷The third time he said to him, "Simon son of John, do you love me?"

Peter was hurt because Jesus asked him the third time, "Do you love me?" He said, "Lord, you know all things; you know that I love you."

¹⁸Jesus said, "Feed my sheep. I tell you the truth, when you were

younger you dressed yourself and went where you wanted; but when you are old you will stretch out your hands, and someone else will dress you and lead you where you do not want to go." [19]Jesus said this to indicate the kind of death by which Peter would glorify God. Then he said to him, "Follow me!"

[20]Peter turned and saw that the disciple whom Jesus loved was following them. (This was the one who had leaned back against Jesus at the supper and had said, "Lord, who is going to betray you?") [21]When Peter saw him, he asked, "Lord, what about him?"

[22]Jesus answered, "If I want him to remain alive until I return, what is that to you? You must follow me." [23]Because of this, the rumor spread among the brothers that this disciple would not die. But Jesus did not say that he would not die; he only said, "If I want him to remain alive until I return, what is that to you?"

[24]This is the disciple who testifies to these things and who wrote them down. We know that his testimony is true.

[25]Jesus did many other things as well. If every one of them were written down, I suppose that even the whole world would not have room for the books that would be written.

Read 1 Peter 5:8-11.

[8]Be self-controlled and alert. Your enemy the devil prowls around like a roaring lion looking for someone to devour. [9]Resist him, standing firm in the faith, because you know that your brothers throughout the world are undergoing the same kind of sufferings.

[10]And the God of all grace, who called you to his eternal glory in Christ, after you have suffered a little while, will himself restore you and make you strong, firm and steadfast. [11]To him be the power forever and ever. Amen.

1. What visual images from John 21 stand out in your mind?

2. What examples do you see in John 21 of Christ's kindness?

3. What evidences do you see in this chapter of Simon Peter's loyalty to Jesus?

4. If you had been Peter, what would you find difficult about this conversation with Jesus?

5. When have you experienced a time of restoration with God?

What continued influence has this restoration had on your life?

6. Focus on 1 Peter 5:8-11. What changes do these words reflect in Peter's character?

7. What personal encouragement do you find in these closing words to Peter's first letter?

8. As you look back over your own history with Christ, what changes do you see him making in your character?

9. As part of his restoration Jesus asked Simon Peter three times, "Do you love me?" How would you answer that question?

What specific actions should you take based on your answer?

 COMMIT

■ At a time when other people were leaving Jesus, when Peter may also have had good reason to stop following Jesus, Peter declared his faith. He said, "Lord, to whom shall we go? You have the words of eternal life" (John 6:68). Meditate on Peter's words as you reflect on your own temptations to turn away. Talk to God about your temptations to stray but also about your commitment to him.

■ Peter was a natural leader whom Jesus trained to become a spiritual leader. But he also became a follower—a loyal follower of Jesus. Reflect on the natural abilities to lead and to follow that God has given you. Pray about how he might be refining those abilities as he shapes you into an effective servant in his kingdom.

■ Read other biblical accounts of Peter's life and writings, for example: Luke 5:1-11; Matthew 14:22-36; John 6:53-71; Matthew 16:13-20; John 13:1-38; Acts 2:1-47; 1 and 2 Peter.

Pray, including expressions of your love and commitment to Jesus, any reservations about the extent of your love, and ways that you hope to do the work of showing love to Jesus and to his people.

For further reading: *Chapter seven of* Never Beyond Hope.

GUIDELINES FOR LEADERS

Leading a Bible discussion can be an enjoyable and rewarding experience. But it can also be intimidating—especially if you've never done it before. If this is how you feel, you're in good company.

Remember when God asked Moses to lead the Israelites out of Egypt? Moses replied, "O Lord, please send someone else to do it" (Ex 4:13). But God gave Moses the help (human and divine) he needed to be a strong leader.

Leading a Bible discussion is not difficult if you follow certain guidelines. You don't need to be an expert on the Bible or a trained teacher. The suggestions listed below can help you to effectively fulfill your role as leader—and enjoy doing it.

PREPARING FOR THE STUDY

1. As you study the passage ahead of time, ask God to help you understand it and apply it in your own life. Unless this happens, you will not be prepared to lead others. Pray too for the various members of the group. Ask God to open your hearts to the message of his Word and motivate you to action.

2. Read the introduction to the entire guide to get an overview of the subject at hand and the issues that will be explored.

3. Be ready for the "Open" questions with a personal story or example. The group will be only as vulnerable and open as its leader.

4. Read the chapter of the companion book that is suggested under "Further Reading" at the end of each study.

5. As you begin preparing for each study, read and reread the assigned Bible passage to familiarize yourself with it. You may want to look up the passage in a Bible so that you can see its context.

6. This study guide is based on the New International Version of the Bible. That is what is reproduced in your guide. It will help you and the group if you use this translation as the basis for your study and discussion.

7. Carefully work through each question in the study. Spend time in meditation and reflection as you consider how to respond.

8. Write your thoughts and responses in the space provided in the study guide. This will help you to express your understanding of the passage clearly.

9. It might help you to have a Bible dictionary handy. Use it to look up any unfamiliar words, names or places.

10. Take the final (application) questions and the "Commit" portion of each study seriously. Consider what this means for your life, what changes you may need to make in your lifestyle and/or what actions you can take in your church or with people you know. Remember that the group will follow your lead in responding to the studies.

LEADING THE STUDY

1. Be sure everyone in your group has a study guide and Bible. Encourage the group to prepare beforehand for each discussion by reading the introduction to the guide and by working through the questions in the study.

2. At the beginning of your first time together, explain that these studies are meant to be discussions, not lectures. Encourage the members of the group to participate. However, do not put pressure on those who may be hesitant to speak during the first few sessions.

3. Begin the study on time. Open with prayer, asking God to help the group understand and apply the passage.

4. Have a group member read the introductory paragraph at the beginning of the discussion. This will remind the group of the topic of the study.

5. Every study begins with a section called "Open." These "approach" questions are meant to be asked before the passage is read. They are important for several reasons.

   First, there is always a stiffness that needs to be overcome before people will begin to talk openly. A good question will break the ice.

   Second, most people will have lots of different things going on in their minds (dinner, an exam, an important meeting coming up, how to get the car fixed) that have nothing to do with the study. A creative question will get their attention and draw them into the discussion.

   Third, approach questions can reveal where our thoughts or feelings need to be transformed by Scripture. That is why it is especially important not to read the passage before the approach question is asked. The passage will tend to color the honest reactions people would otherwise give, because they feel they are supposed to think the way the Bible does.

6. Have a group member read aloud the passage to be studied.

7. As you ask the questions, keep in mind that they are designed to be used just as they are written. You may simply read them aloud. Or you may prefer to express them in your own words.

   There may be times when it is appropriate to deviate from the study guide. For example, a question may already have been answered. If so, move on to the next question. Or someone may raise an important question not covered in the guide. Take time to discuss it, but try to keep the group from going off on tangents.

8. Avoid answering your own questions. Repeat or rephrase them if necessary until they are clearly understood. An eager group quickly becomes passive and silent if members think the leader will give all the *right* answers.

9. Don't be afraid of silence. People may need time to think about the question before formulating their answers.

10. Don't be content with just one answer. Ask, "What do the rest of you think?" or, "Anything else?" until several people have given answers to a question.

11. Acknowledge all contributions. Be affirming whenever possible. Never reject an answer. If it is clearly off-base, ask, "Which verse led you to that conclusion?" or, "What do the rest of you think?"

12. Don't expect every answer to be addressed to you, even though this will probably happen at first. As group members become more at ease, they will begin to truly interact with each other. This is one sign of healthy discussion.

13. Don't be afraid of controversy. It can be stimulating! If you don't resolve an issue completely, don't be frustrated. Move on and keep it in mind for later. A subsequent study may solve the problem.

14. Periodically summarize what the group has said about the passage. This helps to draw together the various ideas mentioned and gives continuity to the study. But don't preach.

15. Don't skip over the application questions at the end of each study. It's important that we each apply the message of the passage to ourselves in a specific way. Be willing to get things started by describing how you have been affected by the study.

Depending on the makeup of your group and the length of time you've been together, you may or may not want to discuss the "Commit" section. If not, allow the group to read it and reflect on it silently. Encourage members to make specific commitments and to write them in their study guide. Ask them the following week how they did with their commitments.

16. Conclude your time together with conversational prayer. Ask for God's help in following through on the commitments you've made.

17. End on time.

Many more suggestions and helps are found in The Big Book on Small Groups *by Jeffrey Arnold.*

Study One. **JACOB: HOPE FOR THE UNHAPPY.**
Genesis 32:1-32.

Purpose: To focus on God's purposes rather than our own pursuit of happiness.

Question 1. When night falls, Jacob breaks up the gift he has planned. He splits his own flocks and herds, from which he has already taken a large gift for Esau, and he sends them ahead separately. He wants to make these flocks and their shepherds into a series of distinct signs of the wealth he brings and from which he may well, in the future, give Esau more. He hopes all of this will mollify Esau before Esau meets him. But as a realist he is providing for the worst case: if Esau attacks one group, the rest, being separate, may escape (v. 8). Then he sends his wives and their maidservants and his eleven sons across the ford of the Jabbok. Now he is left alone.

Question 2. Genesis 32:9-12 tells us that Jacob prayed. He invokes God's faithfulness thus far and makes this the basis for his plea that God will continue to watch over him—because God is his only hope. Jacob knows that. This is perhaps the most desperate prayer he's ever made. It deserves detailed study.

Question 6. Jacob called the place Peniel, which means "face of God," for he realized that he had experienced what we call a theophany, a manifestation of God to him: "I saw God face to face." What do we make of that? We may not experience a wrestling match as Jacob did, but God always appears to people in the form in which it will most help them to meet him—as an indestructible burning bush to Moses, as a soldier to Joshua, as an enthroned monarch to Isaiah and Ezekiel. And here God appears as a wrestler, forcing Jacob to the ground.

Question 7. What this wrestling match shows us is that God has to bring us down before he can raise us up. Down from what? Down from the way that we set ourselves up in pride, self-sufficiency, cleverness, initiative, self-reliance and conscious adversarial tactics so that we can outsmart other people. This had been Jacob's way, and now all his self-serving habits were being squeezed out of him. That's what God was doing as he wrestled with Jacob. Rebekah's spoiled boy needed this treatment and needed it badly. However, let us be clear that original sin, the deepest root of pride and self-serving, is a universal disease, and we all need the same treatment to some extent. Because Jacob had a heart for God as well as for gain, God mercifully guided him, guarded him and changed him for the better. The change process was, however, traumatic and left him permanently lame. Other proud hearts may need comparable treatment today, and God one way or another may give it. It will be an act of grace if and when he does, however low we may be brought in the process.

Question 9. We serve a God who loves us, and we're to interpret everything that happens to us in terms of the love of God. But if perhaps we feel that we have failed our God, we must remember that as Christians we live by being forgiven. Our God is endlessly gracious. We must confess our follies, receive his forgiveness and then look to him to help us forward. As there was recovery first for Jacob and then for his family, so there is hope in God for us and ours.

Study Two.   MANOAH'S WIFE:
              HOPE FOR THE IGNORED. Judges 13:1-25.
              Purpose: To prepare for surprises from God.

Question 2. If you put yourself in the situation of Manoah and his wife, you will find much to bring both fright and joy. Practical reasons for both emotions appear throughout the story. On a theological level, part of this confusing blend of emotions comes from the mystery of God. Manoah asked the name of their visitor, and the visitor did not give an answer—or rather he gave an answer that was quite unclear, something to the effect of, "There is more to me than ever you can understand, and I'm not telling you my name so as to help you realize that." Shortly we find Manoah saying, "We have seen God!" I think the theologians (and Manoah) are right to suppose that this *angel* (the term means "messenger" in both Hebrew and Greek) was a preincarnate appearance of the Son of God, the personal divine Word whom we know as Jesus Christ our Lord.

Question 4. A paraphrase of verse 8 might have Manoah saying, "You know, Lord, I can't rely on the things she says, and this is important. Please let the man of God come to me and tell me what we're to do. Then I'll see to it that we obey instructions." Interesting that God's response to that prayer was a return visit—to the woman. By the end of the account, it is the woman who brings solid sense and aggressive faith to the dilemma. Perhaps Manoah needed her more than the initial scenes of the story suggest.

Question 5. Manoah's response to God's startling surprise might be likely for many of us. "We are doomed to die! We have seen God!" Manoah had hold of a half-truth at this point. He realized that neither he nor his wife was fit by nature to fellowship with God. What is reflected in Manoah's words was his sense that God is, in truth, *holy*: pure, just, strong, intolerably severe, terrifyingly hostile to evil and imperfection, and inexorable once he detects things that are wrong. There's a truth there—although it was a superstitious panic that Manoah was expressing. What Manoah said here shows that his religion was only skin-deep, a formality based on fear rather than a fellowship based on faith. Under similar unnerving circumstances and traumatic troubles, we might say the same. We might think that God has turned against us. We say, "I thought God would protect me and give me a sheltered life, but I was wrong. He cannot love me after all. All my hope is gone." Manoah's wife, on the other hand, shows in her response to Manoah's fear that she is a truly spiritual person with a heart firmly anchored in God himself, a depth that her husband lacks. In this story, Mrs. Manoah is a more appropriate model for our own faith.

Question 6. Look for ways that God is revealing himself in verses 16-20. What do his words and actions suggest about his nature, purpose and plan? If we could listen to an elongated version of this husband-wife conversation, recorded in verses 22-23, we might hear Manoah's wife say something like this: "Manoah, if the LORD had meant to kill us here and now, he would not have accepted a burned offering or a grain offering from our hand, and he has in fact just accepted both. He would not in that case have shown us all these things that he has now shown us, nor told us that we're going to have a son. That certainly means that, far from killing us, he is instead going to keep us alive for nine months at least. He's perfectly consistent. He stands by his purposes; he fulfills his promises. Our God is God the faithful One, wise, steady and safe for us to trust, and that's what we must hold on to as we seek to get our breath back after what we have seen." Manoah and his wife did not learn all of this from a single encounter with God; they drew on it as they coped with one of God's surprises. What they knew about God helped them accept what they could not know—and continue to trust him.

Question 7. Consider some of the mystifying events in your own life—and God's hand in them. Consider also some of the mysteries embedded in his character: his wrath and mercy, his holiness and grace, his timelessness but his entering time with the birth of Christ.

Study Three.   JONAH: HOPE FOR THE ANGRY. Jonah 1—4.

Purpose: To cultivate mercy in ourselves—as God is merciful.

Open. Spend a few moments of silence searching your heart for appropriate responses to these questions. If you are leading a group, suggest a couple of areas to consider. As you bring these two settings into your own framework, you will be ready to see yourself in Jonah—and in Nineveh.

Question 1. The biblical texts show that Jonah was prophet but also a merciless, uncaring man. He was a Jew in the Northern Kingdom in the days of Jeroboam II, whose military success in restoring Israel's former boundaries Jonah had been privileged to predict (1 Kings 14:25). He clearly was a patriot whose affection was focused on his own people. Nineveh was the capital of Assyria, a large city in a large nation. In Jonah's day (the eighth century before Christ) its size, influence and military might made it the leading imperial power of the day and a constant threat to the Jews of Israel. But Jonah is at least an honest man. He spells out in his prayers exactly how he feels about the way God has acted. He hates to think of the use God has made of his own prophetic ministry, and in his disgust he tells God that he would rather be dead than alive (Jonah 4:3). Jonah is also an angry man, angry at God, letting his anger overflow against God for what God has done.

Question 2. One of the interesting things in the book of Jonah is that nearly every time God is spoken of, he is referred to by the covenant name that he had give to the Jews—the name whereby they were to invoke him, and terms of which were to love and trust him. That name used to be rendered Jehovah; scholars now pronounce it Yahweh. In our English translations it's the LORD (in small caps). In this book of forty-eight verses the name appears twenty-six times. Yet this great God Jehovah reveals himself throughout this book as a God of grace and mercy. First, the effect of stilling the storm is that the crew "greatly feared the LORD, and they offered a sacrifice to the LORD, and made vows to him" (v. 16). This is an Old Testament way of saying that they were converted through the work of the Holy Spirit in their hearts. They had really come to know and serve the real God. That was mercy from God to this pagan crew. Second, God showed mercy to Nineveh. He moved in their hearts just as he had moved in the hearts of the pagan crew and so we read in verse 5, "The Ninevites believed God." The king himself calls Nineveh to repentance. God's grace to Nineveh seems disgraceful to Jonah, a soft-hearted lapse from what he thought God ought to be doing, and Jonah's running away to Tarshish had really been the prophet's attempt to save God from himself. But God was merciful even to his reluctant and angry prophet. "Have you any right to be angry?" God asks (4:4). Jonah in his own conscience knows, or half-knows, that by this question God is rebuking him. It's mercy that God doesn't let us ignore that prodding of our consciences.

Question 3. Jonah's two prayers are full of profound spiritual insight. Yet he (like we) failed to live up to what he believed to be true of God. For example, the Hebrew says in 1:3, that Jonah went out from God's *presence*. The presence of the Lord is something very precious. It is not a geographical but a covenantal reality. It is, precisely, knowing that God is with you to bless you wherever you are. When Jonah ran away from the Lord in disobedience, I think he knew that he was running away from the blessing of God. It was a sort of spiritual suicide. But I suppose he thought of it as a brave gesture. He didn't want any chance of Nineveh repenting; he wanted Nineveh to be judged. The happiest thing for Israel, he thought, would be to see Assyria go up in flames; so he defies God by refusing to preach there. He saw himself as a hero, sacrificing himself for his people's welfare. But it was idiocy, really. He was leaving the presence of the Lord. He was turning his back on God, and God on his throne in glory will not have his purposes thwarted by action like this.

Question 5. The fish is one of God's many mercies to Jonah. The Lord prepared the great fish to swallow Jonah up, but he didn't lose consciousness straightaway. When he found himself inside the fish, spiritually he came to his senses. Thoughts went through his mind, and humble, hopeful, thankful, trustful prayer came out of his heart—which (later, one supposes) he turned into the psalm in Jonah 2:1-9. Soon we read, "The LORD commanded the fish, and it vomited Jonah onto dry land." It was not just that God had saved Jonah's life. God had shown his hand; God had taught his prophet a lesson; God had opened his heart; God had forgiven him for a ruinous bit of disobedience; God had restored him to godliness and now wished to restore him to his prophetic ministry. Awed at that moment by the marvel of God's majestic mercy, Jonah must surely have resolved never to say no to God again.

Question 9. God taught Jonah two key lessons: the lesson of obedience and the lesson of compassion. These are lessons our Lord wants each of us to learn. As you and I live by being forgiven, as the Ninevites lived by being forgiven, and as Jonah himself lived by being forgiven, so let us appreciate God's saving mercy, which both lessons presuppose. As God taught Jonah the necessity of obedience in his service, so let us allow him to sensitize our consciences to the importance of always doing what he commands. As God set himself to change Jonah into a man of compassion, so let us allow him to teach us to be men and women of compassion, neighbor lovers in the fullest sense.

Whenever you feel hostile to anybody or any group of people, however badly they may have behaved toward you, stop and remember, and say to yourself: God made them, as God made me. God loves them, as God loves me. If they turn to Christ, they'll be forgiven, as I am forgiven. It's not my part to cherish hostility toward them because of what I see as their sins when my Savior-God has shown such wonderful redemptive love toward sinful me. This is an element in the Christian mindset that you learn to experience, by making yourself think along these lines. Namely, love your enemies as well as your friends, and desire God's best for the one category as well as the other. Loving your neighbor includes enemies as well as friends. It's a tremendous lesson, and it takes all of life for some of us to learn it.

Let us learn also from Jonah how ruinous a thing it is to defy God and imagine that we can get away with refusing to do his will. God is in his heaven; God is on the throne; God is fully in charge of his world. No one can get away with defying God.

Study Four. **MARTHA: HOPE FOR THE OVERWORKED.**
Luke 10:38-42; John 11:1-44; 12:1-3.
Purpose: To express our discipleship to Jesus through work and through devotion (which ever is appropriate for the setting), and to do both with contentment.

Open. We need Marthas in our lives. Without their practical work, nothing would get done. We'd live our whole existence on thoughts and feelings—and soon starve. Sometimes we rightly take Martha roles ourselves. Some of us are good at it, and God uses our hands-on skills and dedicated work. But we, like Martha, have to learn that when we are sharing our lives with our Lord Jesus Christ, we are not in charge. He's in charge. As we follow Martha through the three scenes where the Gospels show her in action, we shall see her learning this lesson.

When we say to the Lord Jesus, "I'm glad you are in my life—but remember, I'm in charge," we forfeit much blessing and rob God of much glory if we take that line. Martha's story should point us in a different direction. As for Mary, we need her too. In the end (for this particular occasion) we hear Jesus say to fretting Martha, "Martha, Martha, you are worried and upset about many things, but only one thing is needed. Mary has chosen what is better. And it will not be taken from her" (Lk 10:41-42).

Question 2. The first thing communicated by Martha's words was that she wanted to be noticed. Jesus' reply to her begins, "Martha, Martha, you are worried and upset about many things." In other words: "Martha, you are noticed. I know what you're doing, and I'm grateful. Don't be in any doubt about that." The second thing Martha had expressed was that she wanted to control Mary's life by hauling her out into the kitchen. To that, Jesus' response is, "Mary has chosen what is better, and it will not be taken away from her." This is to say, "Martha, resenting Mary's absence from the kitchen is an attitude you shouldn't have; hauling her there is something you shouldn't be trying to do. You ought to be glad that Mary has the opportunity to sit here and listen to me and learn from me. You should think of it as your gift to her." The third thing that Martha had expressed in her words, as was said above, was a desire to manipulate and use Jesus as her tool against her sibling—in other words, her hammer for hitting Mary over the head. On that, Jesus is being quite firm with Martha. "Martha, you must not try to do that." This is what he implies when he says, "Only one thing is needed. Mary has chosen that good thing, and it will not be taken away from her." (I am not going to order her into the kitchen.)

Question 5. Trace the conversation that Jesus initiated with Martha and the way he guided Martha toward her powerful statement of faith (v. 27). You will find steps toward faith in each verse. In his conversation on the road with Martha, Jesus makes one of the most revealing statements about himself that Scripture records. Clearly he did not hold her previous work in the kitchen against her. When the time was right, Martha received his undivided attention and an intimate revelation of his true nature and purpose. Mary listened at his feet with the disciples; Martha got her own private tutoring session.

Question 7. We see two things here. One is that Martha served the meal at her home. She is still the hostess, and she's managing this celebration dinner in Jesus' honor. Thus by her service she exalts him, as now she wants to do more than she wants anything else. The second thing is that when Mary makes an extravagant gesture of adoration to the Lord, whom she loves so deeply, Martha doesn't say a word. Martha accepts that Mary has a right to express her worship of Jesus in her own way, and that it's not for Martha to put Mary down. From Martha's experience with Jesus we may learn that Jesus values our entire backstage ministry that few, if any, notice and nobody thanks us for. Perhaps we are tempted sometimes to lose patience because we invest a great deal of ourselves in serving others and nobody seems to care. The proper way to handle that feeling is to say, "But Jesus knows and Jesus cares." And indeed he does. When we serve others for his sake, we serve him truly, as did Martha at this banquet.

Question 8. Situational responsibilities are not to be ignored for the sake of devotional exercises, any more than vice versa. Martha has been doing the right thing for her in that situation, as has Mary, though they have been doing different things. The lesson that all have to learn is to be Martha and Mary by turn. When the meal was made, it would be right for Martha to come in and join the party, learn from Jesus and deepen her relationship with him—just as Mary was doing. But until the requirements of hospitality were covered, Martha's place was backstage, doing what she had to do as Jesus' hostess.

Question 9. Let's learn that we ought to have space in our lives for doing what Mary did: spending time with the Word of God, learning from Jesus by listening to him in worship and adoration—which is the most important activity of our lives. But let us also learn that from time to time we are to be doing the practical helpful things that are needed around the house and, for that matter, around the church. Let us not suppose that intensity of devotion excuses us from this. Some of us skimp the Martha side of our discipleship, just as some of us skimp our times of Bible reading and prayer—the Mary side of our discipleship. And skimping both ways is wrong. Our Lord Jesus looks for better than that from all of us.

Study Five.   THOMAS: HOPE FOR THE HARD TO CONVINCE. John 20:19-31.

Purpose: *To become convinced (with Thomas) that Jesus is "My Lord and my God."*

Question 3. Jesus' ministry to Thomas is quite simply overwhelming kindness. Thomas had painted himself into a corner, and Jesus affirms him by taking him at his word, meeting him where he is and saying in effect, "If it is going to help you to finger the wounds in my body, then finger them. Only stop acting the unbeliever, Thomas. Acknowledge the reality of my rising. Believe." We're not told whether Thomas actually did what Jesus was inviting him to do. Maybe he stood, bowed, even knelt; we don't know. What is apparent though is that Thomas was absolutely broken. "My Lord, and my God," he said. And in saying that, he made the perfect confession of faith, the fullest and clearest that is found anywhere in the Gospels. It is as if he said, "Lord Jesus, yes I believe. I believe that you are alive from the dead, and I should have believed that a week ago. I honor you now, both for your glorious rising and for your loving ministry to me at this moment. You are God and I should be your person, your servant, your worshiper from now on. And whatever you send in your providence, your ordering of things, I should take as from your hand. I should recognize that henceforth I'll never be out of your sight but shall always be in your fellowship. I didn't believe that before, but I believe it now." As in marriage, so here: vows confirm a permanent commitment. Here and now I vow to be yours, Lord. And Thomas's statement of faith was a vow, "Jesus, you are my Lord and my God."

Question 4. As you look at four potential obstacles to Thomas's faith, you may spot similar forces on your own life or personality. First Thomas may have been depressive. (Other biblical texts suggest this possibility.) When I say this, I am not thinking of people in pathological and clinical depression, whom medication and psychiatry can help, but of the temperamental depressives (the Eeyores and Puddleglums) of the human race. Their minds are anchored in gloom and despondency. Second, I think stress had something to do with his attitude. By the time Jesus' body was taken down from the cross, the disciples had been through an awful lot. They were utterly crushed and totally at a loss. Thomas had been with them throughout, and Thomas (because of his temperament, I imagine) made heavier weather of it than the rest of them. Perhaps the reason why Thomas was not with the ten when Jesus first came was that he had gotten beyond the point where he could enjoy being with anyone. Third is pride. Thomas says to his friends, in effect, "Now wait a minute. You're telling me you saw Jesus. All right, that's what you say. But we need solid evidence—at least I do. You didn't touch him, did you? Haven't you ever heard of people who've seen visions and there wasn't anything really there? If I'd been with you, I would have insisted on touching him." Fourth, resentment might also have had something to do with Thomas's reaction of unbelief. Thomas could have been expressing his resentment of the fact that Jesus had come to the ten and hadn't come to him. They had received a blessing that he himself had missed, and he resented that whole situation and his rejection of what his friends were saying was a way of expressing that resentment.

Question 7. There is every reason to believe that Jesus rose from the dead. The original disciples bore witness. They preached the gospel, brought people of many nationalities to faith, founded churches and wrote material that now serves to guide all of us in later generations into faith like theirs. Most of the apostles were martyred. All of them were willing to die for Christ. If they had had the slightest doubt as to whether the Christ they preached was for real or if there had been the slightest pretense in the attitude they first adopted, they wouldn't have behaved like that.

They knew, and so they were prepared to give their lives rather than deny or go back on what they knew. Their testimony has come down the centuries to us. And if Jesus didn't rise from the dead, why didn't the Jews at once produce the body from the grave to show that Jesus wasn't risen and that all this talk about resurrection faith was nonsense? The answer is simple: they didn't produce the body because they couldn't produce the body. The body wasn't there; the grave was empty. They knew (as do we) that if Jesus didn't rise from the dead, the whole of Christianity falls apart (1 Cor 15:17-18).

Study Six.   **SIMON PETER: HOPE WHEN I HAVE DONE SOMETHING TERRIBLE.**
John 21:1-25; 1 Peter 5:8-11.
Purpose: To trust the reconciling power of Christ—and then to commit our love to him.

Question 2. Jesus invited Peter to reconciliation with immense kindness. He invited Peter by a threefold profession of love to begin to wash out the bitter memory of that threefold denial. Then each time that Simon said, "Lord, you know that I love you," Jesus immediately gave him a job to do: "Feed my lambs; take care of my sheep; feed my sheep." That was Jesus reinstating Simon in the leadership role in ministry that he had had in mind for his disciples right from the word go. Simon had gone out fishing the night before because he was quite sure that it was all up with his public discipleship and his public ministry. He'd disqualified himself forever from being any use to the Lord Jesus, or so he thought. But here is the Lord Jesus putting him back in that leadership role, specifically recommissioning him for ministry, and the link between Jesus' question to him and the recommissioning is in his words, "Lord, you know that I love you."

Question 3. Reread the chapter, looking particularly at what Peter says and does. Try to trace his thinking, looking for signs of loyalty to Jesus—in spite of his previous actions.

Question 6. Peter's letter, written late in his life, flashes ahead to what Jesus predicted to Peter that morning on the shore. His letter, written to encourage struggling believers, is full of suffering, but beyond that it is full of faith that endures suffering—and still believes. On the shore that post-Easter morning, Jesus pulls aside for a moment the curtain that hides the future. He tells Simon in effect that the disciples are going to finish their ministry by being martyred for the glory of God.

I think Jesus did that because he wanted to give Simon an opportunity to negate in an explicit way that panicky passion to save his own skin, which had led to the denial. So Jesus tells him bluntly, "Simon, if you accept my recommissioning, you won't be able to save your skin. I want you to know that. You will glorify me finally by death, a martyr's death, at the hands of the authorities, who will execute you as a subversive, just as they did to me. Now, against the background of that, Simon, I say to you, 'Follow me.'" Simon Peter did just that—to the end.

Question 9. We need to be honest with ourselves and with God if the hope of God remaking us as he remade Simon is to be fulfilled. Can we say to Jesus with Simon Peter, "Lord, you know that I love you"? No doubt we are compelled to say with him, "Lord I know I've let you down. What I have done is terrible, and the memory of it is awful—and yet in my heart I do love you, and what I want more than anything is to love you more and better." Have we heard the voice of Jesus speaking pardon and peace to our hearts for our sins and failures, assuring us that despite everything, he still has work for us to do? Have we heard him telling us that the way to show love to anyone—to our Lord himself, to other Christians, to our own nearest and dearest, or whomever—is by what we do for them, over and above anything we say to them? Becoming this honest, realistic and responsive to the Son of God was, as we have seen, the path of Simon's progress. It was how he came to know God the Father. It was as he traveled this path that God transformed him from Simon the unstable into Peter the rock. This is the way you and I must go. May the Lord lead us this way.

COMMITMENT

May 14th { My Heart - God's Home
by Munger